WELCOME TO THE U.S.A.
MAINE

BUOYS
LARGE 8.95 SMALL 4.95

Written by Ann Heinrichs   Illustrated by Matt Kania
Content Adviser: Jim Brunelle, Author and Editor
of Maine Almanac, Cape Elizabeth, Maine

Published in the United States of America by The Child's World®
PO Box 326 • Chanhassen, MN 55317-0326
800-599-READ • www.childsworld.com

Photo Credits
Cover: Digital Vision; frontispiece: Judy Griesedieck/Corbis.

Interior: Renee Armstrong/Fort Fairfield Chamber of Commerce: 25; Bettmann/
Corbis: 10; Burnham Tavern Museum Committee: 13; Getty Images: 14 (Taxi/
Gene Ahrens), 26 (Stone/Donovan Reese); Katahdin Times, Millinocket: 33;
Madawaska Chamber of Commerce: 30; Maine Lobster Festival: 21; Maine
Office of Tourism: 6, 9, 18, 22; Photodisc: 17; Jeffrey Stevenson: 34; Thomas
Moser Cabinetmakers: 29.

Acknowledgments
The Child's World®: Mary Berendes, Publishing Director

Editorial Directions, Inc.: E. Russell Primm, Editorial Director; Katie Marsico, Associate
Editor; Judith Shiffer, Assistant Editor; Matt Messbarger, Editorial Assistant; Susan
Hindman, Copy Editor; Melissa McDaniel, Proofreader; Kevin Cunningham, Peter
Garnham, Matt Messbarger, Olivia Nellums, Chris Simms, Molly Symmonds, Katherine
Trickle, Carl Stephen Wender, Fact Checkers; Tim Griffin/IndexServ, Indexer; Cian
Loughlin O'Day, Photo Researcher and Editor

The Design Lab: Kathleen Petelinsek, Design and art production

Library of Congress Cataloging-in-Publication Data
Heinrichs, Ann.
  Maine / by Ann Heinrichs.
    p. cm. — (Welcome to the U.S.A.)
  Includes index.
  ISBN 1-59296-444-3 (library bound : alk. paper) 1. Maine—Juvenile literature. I. Title.
  F19.3.H453 2006
  974.1—dc22   2005000520

Ann Heinrichs is the author of more than 100 books for children and young adults. She has also enjoyed successful careers as a children's book editor and an advertising copywriter. Ann grew up in Fort Smith, Arkansas, and lives in Chicago, Illinois.

**About the Author
Ann Heinrichs**

Matt Kania loves maps and, as a kid, dreamed of making them. In school he studied geography and cartography, and today he makes maps for a living. Matt's favorite thing about drawing maps is learning about the places they represent. Many of the maps he has created can be found in books, magazines, videos, Web sites, and public places.

**About the
Map Illustrator
Matt Kania**

On the cover: The Bass Harbor Head is just one of many lighthouses along the coast.
On page one: Lobster buoys are for sale in the town of Wells.

OUR MAINE TRIP

Maine's Nicknames: The Pine Tree State and Vacationland

What will you do in Maine today? Meet sea captains and woodworkers? Tie sailors' knots and eat lobsters? Watch people turn wood into paper? Climb a lighthouse? Or sneak up on moose in the woods?

Why pick and choose? Let's do it all! Just follow the dotted line. Or else skip around. Either way, you're in for a great trip. Just remember—having fun is the Maine thing! Now, buckle up and hang on tight. We're on our way!

WELCOME TO MAINE

As you travel through Maine, watch for all the interesting facts along the way.

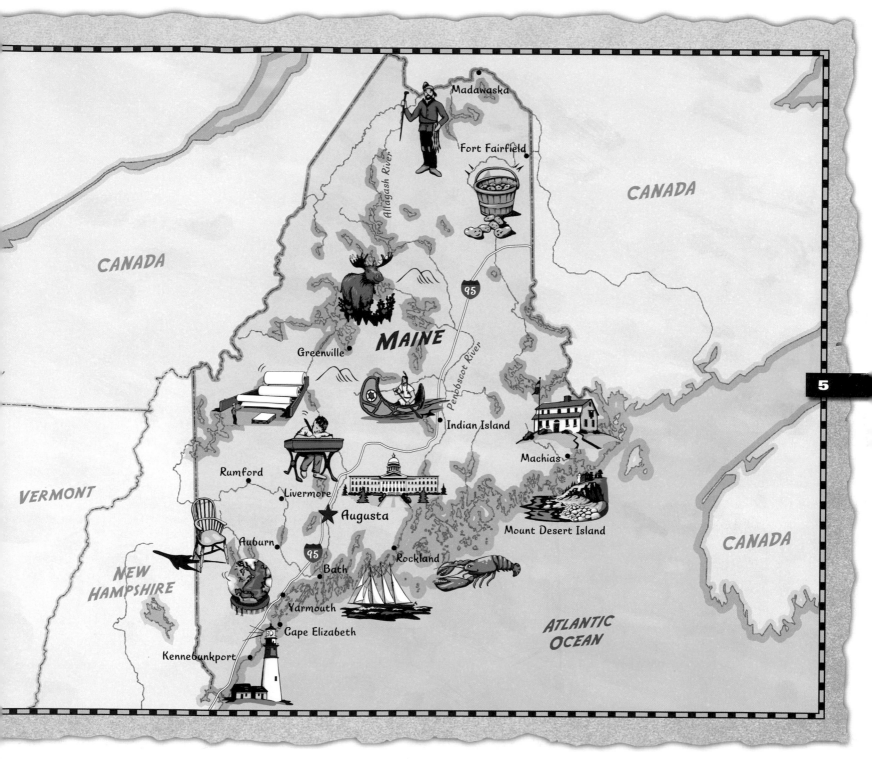

CANADA

CANADA

CANADA

VERMONT

NEW HAMPSHIRE

ATLANTIC OCEAN

MAINE

Madawaska

Fort Fairfield

Allagash River

Penobscot River

Greenville

Indian Island

Machias

Mount Desert Island

Rumford

Livermore

Augusta

Auburn

Bath

Rockland

Yarmouth

Cape Elizabeth

Kennebunkport

95

95

5

Ready for a scenic sunset? Just head to Acadia National Park!

West Quoddy Head is the country's easternmost point. Stand there at sunrise. You'll be the 1st person in the country to see the sun come up!

Acadia National Park

Acadia National Park is rough and wild. Just stand on its rocky cliffs. Look out, and there's the sea. Water comes crashing in with a great roar!

Most of this park is on Mount Desert Island. That's one of many islands off the coast. Maine is on the northeastern tip of the country. Southeastern Maine faces the Atlantic Ocean. On the west is the state of New Hampshire. The rest of Maine borders Canada.

Much of Maine's coast is rocky. But there are sandy beaches, too. Little fishing villages lie along the shore. Away from the coast, the land rises higher. Mountains cover much of northwestern Maine.

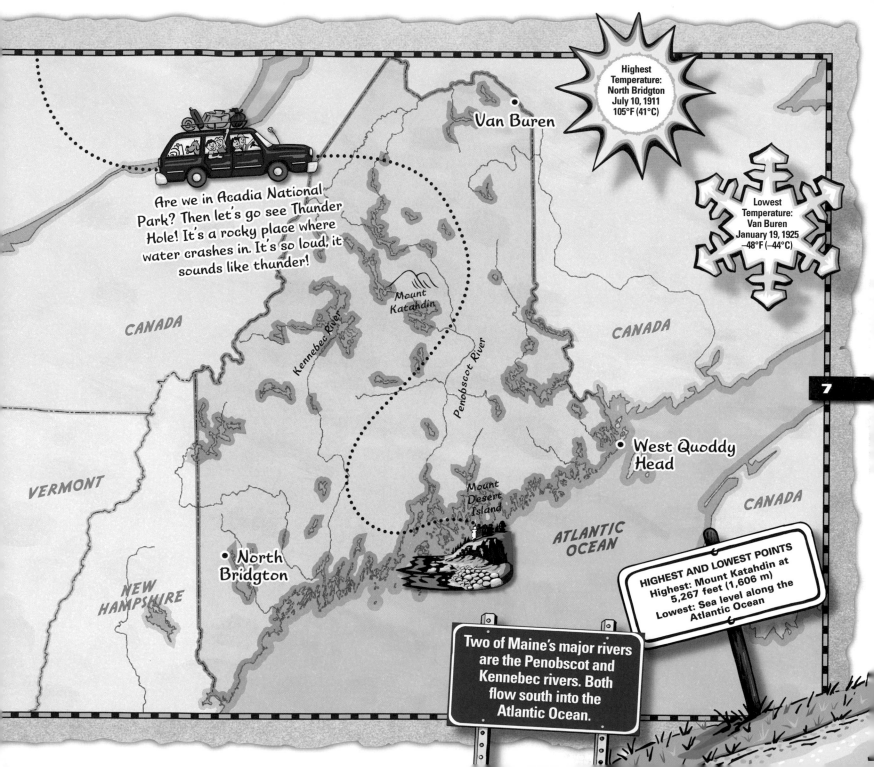

Are we in Acadia National Park? Then let's go see Thunder Hole! It's a rocky place where water crashes in. It's so loud, it sounds like thunder!

Highest Temperature: North Bridgton July 10, 1911 105°F (41°C)

Lowest Temperature: Van Buren January 19, 1925 −48°F (−44°C)

Van Buren

West Quoddy Head

CANADA

CANADA

Mount Katahdin

Kennebec River

Penobscot River

VERMONT

North Bridgton

NEW HAMPSHIRE

Mount Desert Island

ATLANTIC OCEAN

CANADA

HIGHEST AND LOWEST POINTS
Highest: Mount Katahdin at 5,267 feet (1,606 m)
Lowest: Sea level along the Atlantic Ocean

Two of Maine's major rivers are the Penobscot and Kennebec rivers. Both flow south into the Atlantic Ocean.

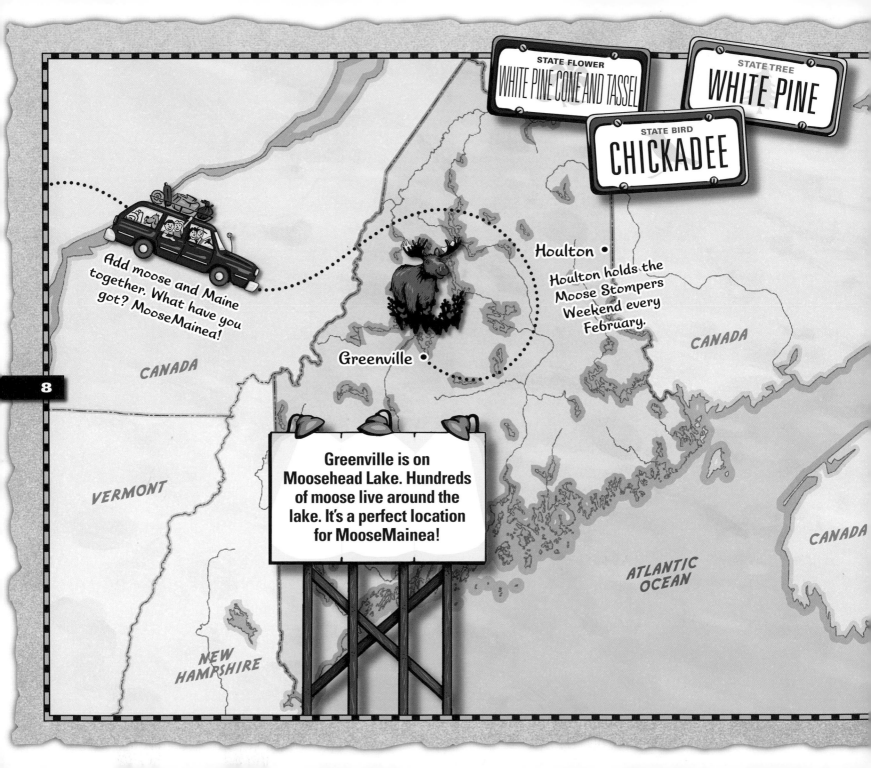

STATE FLOWER
WHITE PINE CONE AND TASSEL

STATE TREE
WHITE PINE

STATE BIRD
CHICKADEE

Add moose and Maine together. What have you got? MooseMainea!

Houlton

Houlton holds the Moose Stompers Weekend every February.

CANADA

CANADA

Greenville

CANADA

Greenville is on Moosehead Lake. Hundreds of moose live around the lake. It's a perfect location for MooseMainea!

VERMONT

NEW HAMPSHIRE

ATLANTIC OCEAN

Take a tour through a moose forest. March in the Moosecapade Parade. Play Pin the Antlers on the Moose. You're celebrating MooseMainea!

MooseMainea honors a beloved Maine animal—the moose! Thousands of big moose live in Maine. Deer, bears, and bobcats live there, too. So do foxes, rabbits, and squirrels.

All these animals have good places to hide. They make their homes in the deep forests. They're lucky to live in Maine. Why? Because forests cover most of the state!

The coastal waters are full of sea life. Lobster and clams are some common shellfish. Maine's fish include Atlantic herring, salmon, cod, and flounder.

This moose makes its home in a Maine forest.

9

The National Park Service has 4 sites in Maine.

This Penobscot Indian is wearing traditional dress.

Many Native American groups once lived in Maine. Some still do. One group is the Penobscot people. How did they live? You'll find out at the Penobscot Nation Museum.

The Penobscot made canoes with birch tree bark. They also made decorated clothes and headdresses for ceremonies. You'll see all these things at the museum.

English settlers sailed to Maine in 1607. They set up the Popham **Colony.** But they left the next year. More **colonists** came in the 1620s and stayed. Maine became part of the Massachusetts Bay Colony.

Colonists and Native Americans fought many battles. Both sides wanted the land as their own. In the end, the colonists won. The Indians were driven out or sent to **reservations.**

The Waponahki Museum is in Perry. It's on the Passamaquoddy Indian Reservation.

10

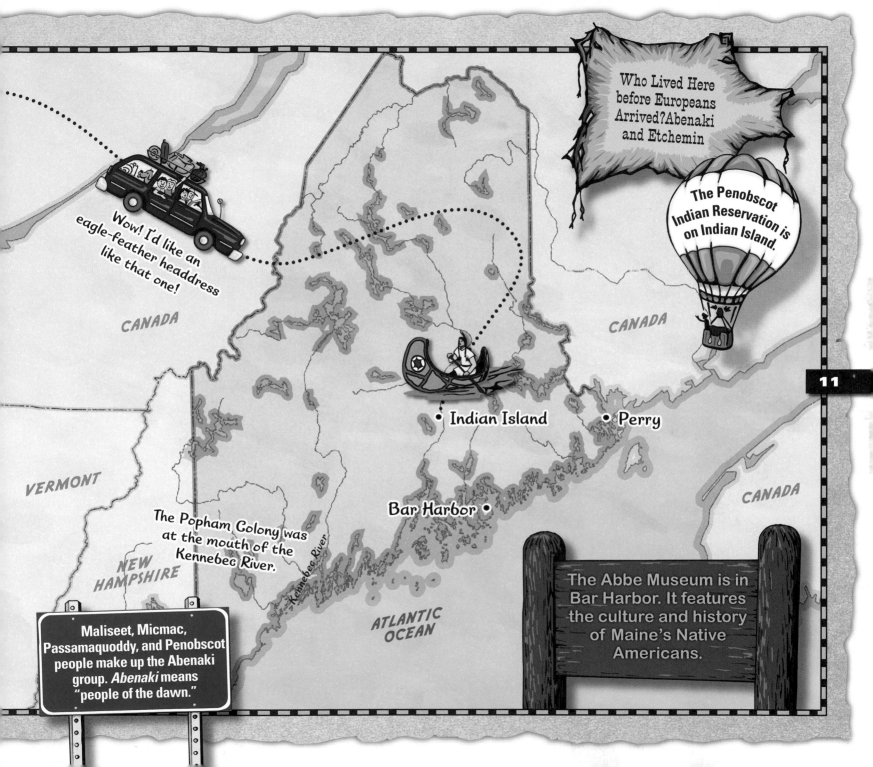

Who Lived Here before Europeans Arrived? Abenaki and Etchemin

The Penobscot Indian Reservation is on Indian Island.

Wow! I'd like an eagle-feather headdress like that one!

CANADA

CANADA

CANADA

VERMONT

NEW HAMPSHIRE

Indian Island

Perry

Bar Harbor

The Popham Colony was at the mouth of the Kennebec River.

Kennebec River

ATLANTIC OCEAN

Maliseet, Micmac, Passamaquoddy, and Penobscot people make up the Abenaki group. Abenaki means "people of the dawn."

The Abbe Museum is in Bar Harbor. It features the culture and history of Maine's Native Americans.

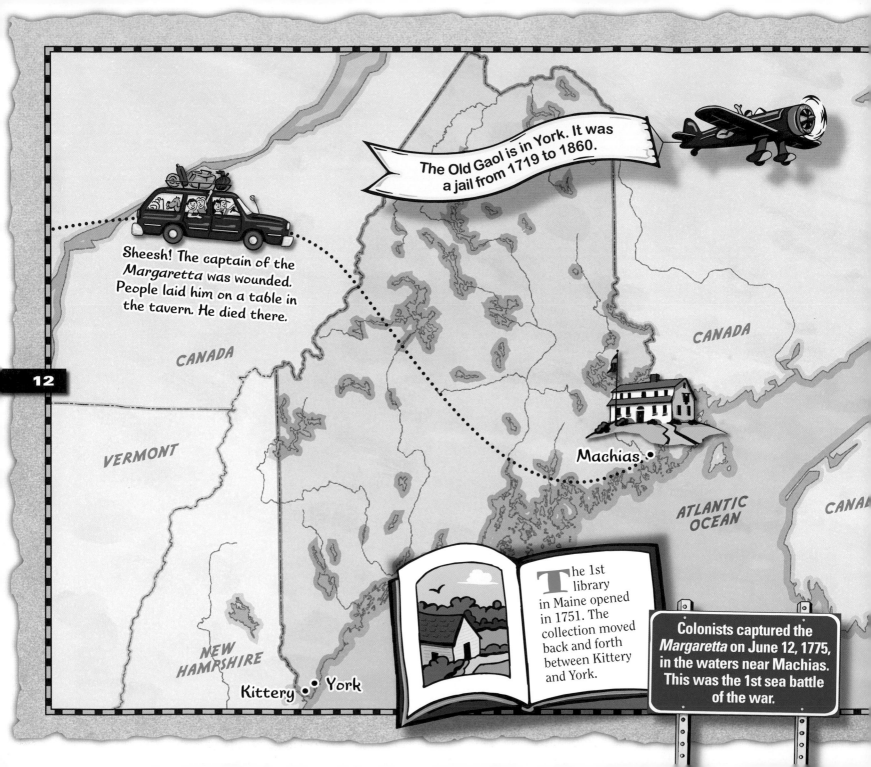

Sheesh! The captain of the Margaretta was wounded. People laid him on a table in the tavern. He died there.

The Old Gaol is in York. It was a jail from 1719 to 1860.

CANADA

CANADA

VERMONT

Machias •

ATLANTIC OCEAN

CANADA

The 1st library in Maine opened in 1751. The collection moved back and forth between Kittery and York.

NEW HAMPSHIRE

Kittery •• York

Colonists captured the Margaretta on June 12, 1775, in the waters near Machias. This was the 1st sea battle of the war.

Burnham Tavern and the Revolutionary War

Thirteen British colonies grew up along North America's Atlantic coast. The colonists came to hate British taxes. They decided to fight for freedom from British rule. This fight is called the Revolutionary War (1775–1783).

One night, colonists met in Machias's Burnham Tavern. They planned to capture the British ship *Margaretta*. And they did! In the end, the colonies won the war. They became the United States of America.

You can visit Burnham Tavern today. You'll see old iron pots by the fireplace. That's where dinners were cooked!

Want to learn about the Revolutionary War? Don't forget to visit Burnham Tavern!

13

14

Maine lawmakers busily work inside the capitol.

Maine used to be part of Massachusetts. But Maine broke away in 1820. At last, it became a state of its own. Portland was the first state capital. But Portland was on the coast. **Politicians** wanted a capital closer to the state's center. They chose Augusta in 1832. There they built the state government building—the capitol.

Inside the capitol are important government offices. Maine's government has three branches. One branch makes state laws. Another branch carries out the laws. It's headed by the governor. The third branch is made up of judges. They decide whether laws have been broken.

Welcome to Augusta, the capital of Maine!

Maine's state motto is *Dirigo*. This is Latin for "I Direct" or "I Guide."

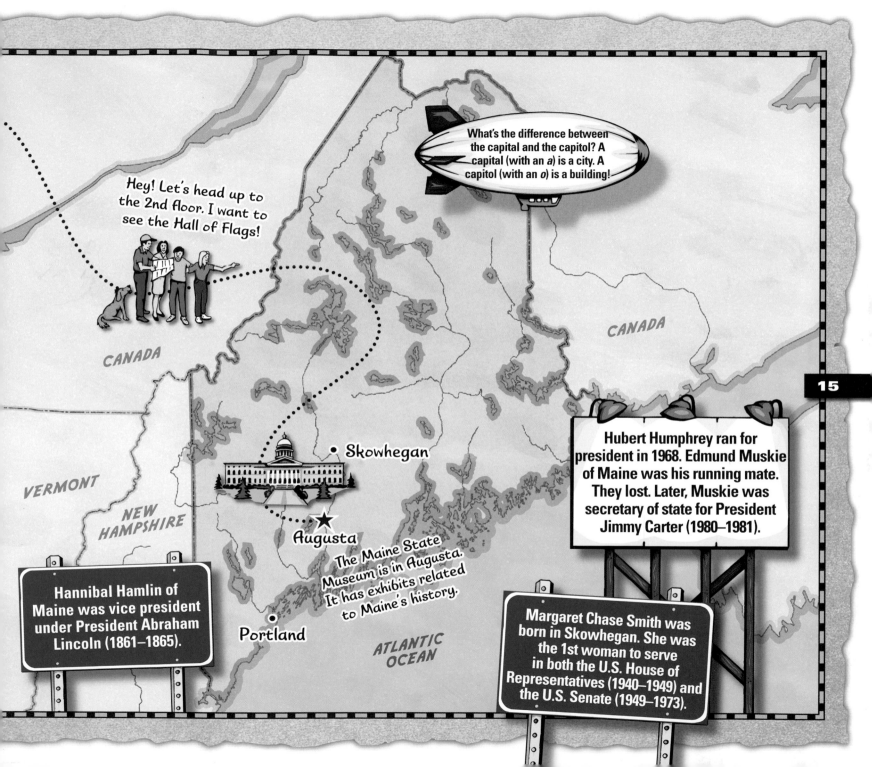

Hey! Let's head up to the 2nd floor. I want to see the Hall of Flags!

What's the difference between the capital and the capitol? A capital (with an *a*) is a city. A capitol (with an *o*) is a building!

CANADA

CANADA

VERMONT

NEW HAMPSHIRE

Skowhegan

★ Augusta

Portland

ATLANTIC OCEAN

The Maine State Museum is in Augusta. It has exhibits related to Maine's history.

Hannibal Hamlin of Maine was vice president under President Abraham Lincoln (1861–1865).

Hubert Humphrey ran for president in 1968. Edmund Muskie of Maine was his running mate. They lost. Later, Muskie was secretary of state for President Jimmy Carter (1980–1981).

Margaret Chase Smith was born in Skowhegan. She was the 1st woman to serve in both the U.S. House of Representatives (1940–1949) and the U.S. Senate (1949–1973).

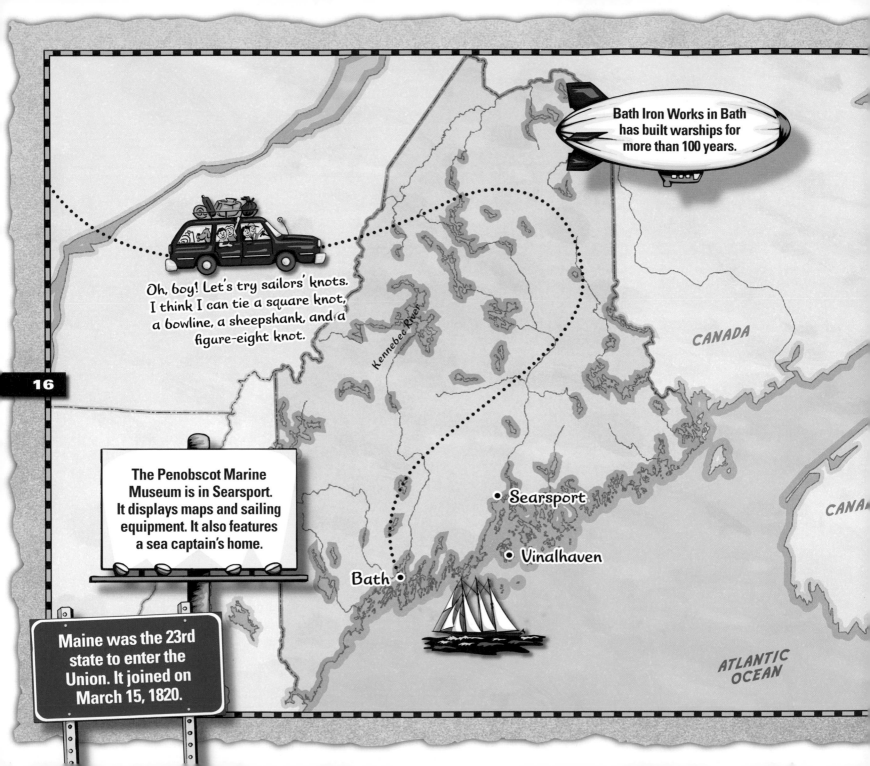

Bath Iron Works in Bath has built warships for more than 100 years.

Oh, boy! Let's try sailors' knots. I think I can tie a square knot, a bowline, a sheepshank, and a figure-eight knot.

CANADA

Kennebec River

The Penobscot Marine Museum is in Searsport. It displays maps and sailing equipment. It also features a sea captain's home.

• Searsport

• Vinalhaven

Bath •

Maine was the 23rd state to enter the Union. It joined on March 15, 1820.

ATLANTIC OCEAN

Do you love ships and the sea? Then you'll love the Maine **Maritime** Museum. You'll learn how Mainers built and sailed ships. You'll try your hand at tying sailors' knots. Go explore the shipyard. Then hop aboard a boat. You'll coast down the Kennebec River.

Fishing and sailing are old **traditions** in Maine. Many Mainers sailed out to sea in big ships. Others sailed smaller boats close to shore. The sailors caught lobsters, fish, and even whales.

Shipbuilding became an important **industry.** The thick pine forests provided wood for the ships. Maine's shipbuilders made sturdy ships for fishing. They also built warships for the U.S. Navy.

Would you make a good fisher? These fishing boats are docked off the coast of Vinalhaven.

17

Portland Head Light guides ships safely to shore. It also serves as a popular tourist attraction.

More than sixty lighthouses rise along Maine's coast. Their lights guide ships safely back to shore. Lighthouse keepers used to tend the lighthouses. They kept lanterns burning in the tower.

Most of Maine's lighthouses still work today. You can climb some of them. Their lights are electric now. Most also have foghorns. The horns blast loudly when it's foggy. Boats can follow the sound back to shore.

Ask Mainers which lighthouse is the most famous. Many will say it's Portland Head Light. It looks out from Cape Elizabeth. Built in 1791, it's Maine's oldest lighthouse.

Nubble Light in York and Pemaquid Point Lighthouse in Bristol are well-known lighthouses.

Boon Island Light near York is Maine's tallest lighthouse. It's 137 feet (42 m) high.

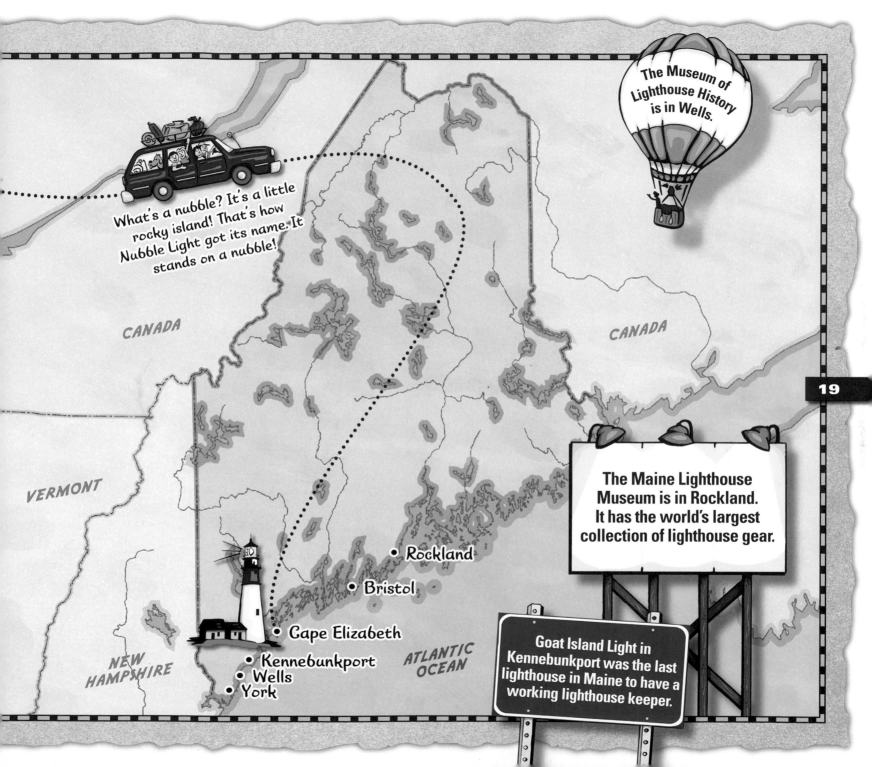

What's a nubble? It's a little rocky island! That's how Nubble Light got its name. It stands on a nubble!

The Museum of Lighthouse History is in Wells.

CANADA

CANADA

VERMONT

The Maine Lighthouse Museum is in Rockland. It has the world's largest collection of lighthouse gear.

• Rockland

• Bristol

• Cape Elizabeth

NEW HAMPSHIRE

• Kennebunkport
• Wells
• York

ATLANTIC OCEAN

Goat Island Light in Kennebunkport was the last lighthouse in Maine to have a working lighthouse keeper.

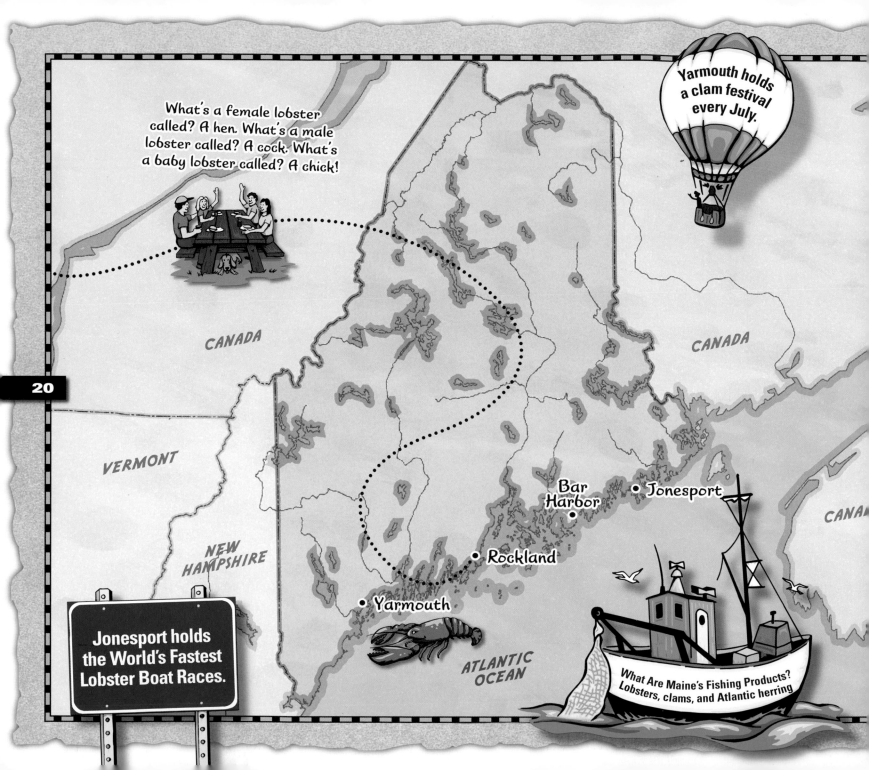

What's a female lobster called? A hen. What's a male lobster called? A cock. What's a baby lobster called? A chick!

Yarmouth holds a clam festival every July.

CANADA

CANADA

CANADA

VERMONT

NEW HAMPSHIRE

Bar Harbor

• Jonesport

• Rockland

• Yarmouth

ATLANTIC OCEAN

Jonesport holds the World's Fastest Lobster Boat Races.

What Are Maine's Fishing Products?
Lobsters, clams, and Atlantic herring

Rockland's Maine Lobster Festival

Are you good at keeping your balance? Then check out the Maine Lobster Festival in Rockland. You could win the lobster crate race! Lobster crates are boxes for holding lobsters.

How does the race work? Lobster crates are tied together in the water. The crates make a kind of race track. Racers run across the crates. Who's the winner? Whoever covers the most crates before falling in!

People eat lots of lobster at this festival. Many other coastal towns have lobster festivals, too. It's no wonder. Maine catches more lobsters than any other state!

Ready, set, go! Check out the lobster crate race in Rockland.

Bar Harbor has the Oceanarium and Lobster Hatchery. You'll see mother and baby lobsters there.

The Living History Center in Livermore

Giddy up! Enjoy a wagon ride at Washburn-Norlands Living History Center.

Many Mainers in the 1800s were farmers. They plowed their fields with ox-drawn plows. They grew crops and raised cows for milk. They gathered maple **sap** and made sugar.

Would you like to see these farm activities? Stop by the Washburn-Norlands Living History Center. You can spend a weekend there. You'll help out with farm chores. You'll even attend classes in the old schoolhouse.

Maine also developed many industries. Mills, or water-powered factories, were built beside rivers. The mills made cotton and wool cloth. Maine was also known for its leather goods.

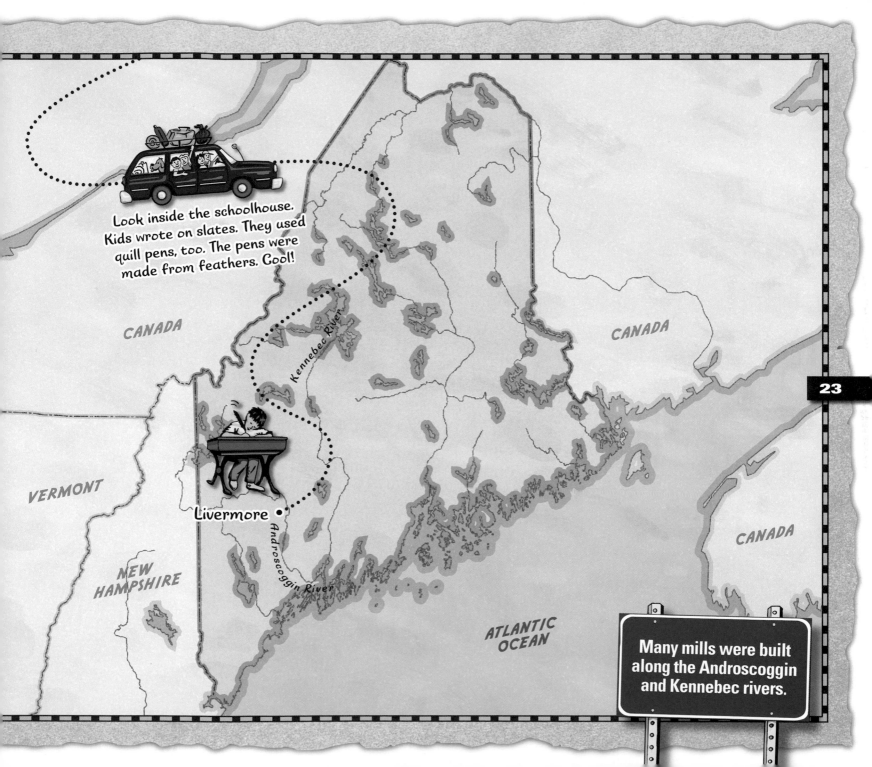

Look inside the schoolhouse. Kids wrote on slates. They used quill pens, too. The pens were made from feathers. Cool!

CANADA

CANADA

CANADA

VERMONT

NEW HAMPSHIRE

Kennebec River

Androscoggin River

Livermore

ATLANTIC OCEAN

Many mills were built along the Androscoggin and Kennebec rivers.

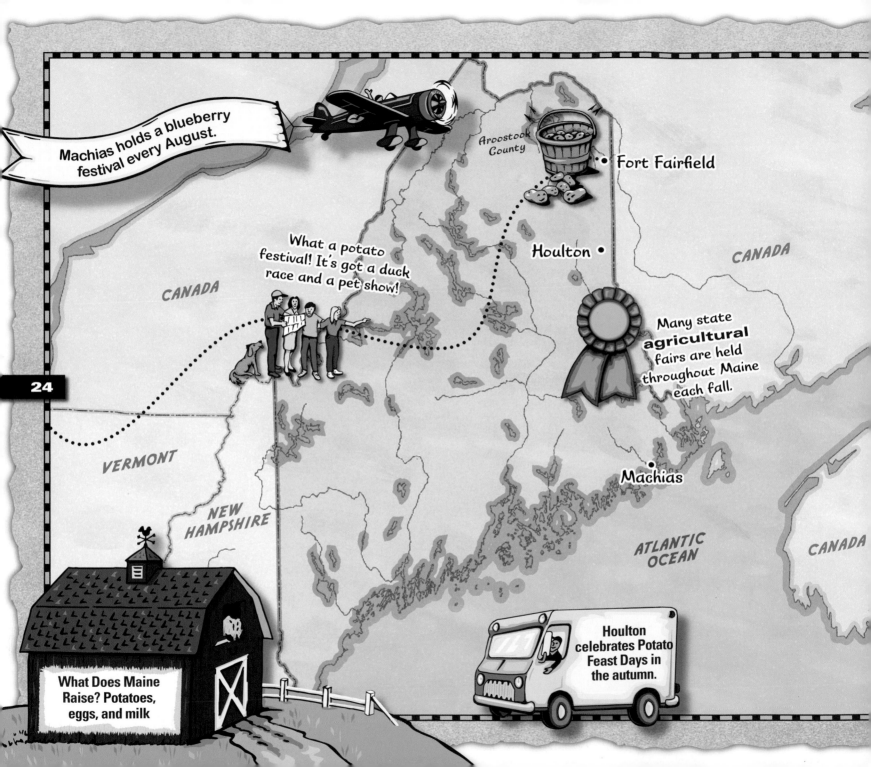

Machias holds a blueberry festival every August.

Aroostook County

Fort Fairfield

What a potato festival! It's got a duck race and a pet show!

CANADA

Houlton

CANADA

Many state **agricultural** fairs are held throughout Maine each fall.

VERMONT

NEW HAMPSHIRE

Machias

ATLANTIC OCEAN

CANADA

What Does Maine Raise? Potatoes, eggs, and milk

Houlton celebrates Potato Feast Days in the autumn.

Fort Fairfield's Potato Blossom Festival

Do you like potatoes? Then check out the Maine Potato Blossom Festival. You can enter the potato-picking contest. Then pick out the yummiest potato recipe. Those cakes and pies are great!

Potatoes are the state's top crop. Maine's potato farmers grow millions of bushels a year!

Apples are Maine's leading fruit. Wild blueberries are important, too. Maine grows more of them than any other state.

What about chickens and cows? Plenty of them live on Maine's farms. Eggs and milk are valuable farm products.

Hop to it! Don't miss the potato sack race in Fort Fairfield.

Most of Maine's potatoes are grown in Aroostook County. That's where Maine's potato festivals are held.

Making Paper in Rumford

Need a new notebook? Perhaps you should visit this paper mill in Houlton.

Many paper mills are at work in Maine. Just stop by Mead Paper in Rumford. Outside, big machines are pushing wood around. Inside, more machines are buzzing away. You'll see how they cut and grind wood. Then they turn wood chips into paper!

Papermaking became a big industry in Maine. Thousands of forest trees now go to paper mills. The mills turn out many products. Can you guess what some of them are?

Paper mills make cardboard boxes and paper sacks. Then there's the paper you write on. And don't forget books and newspapers. They all began as trees!

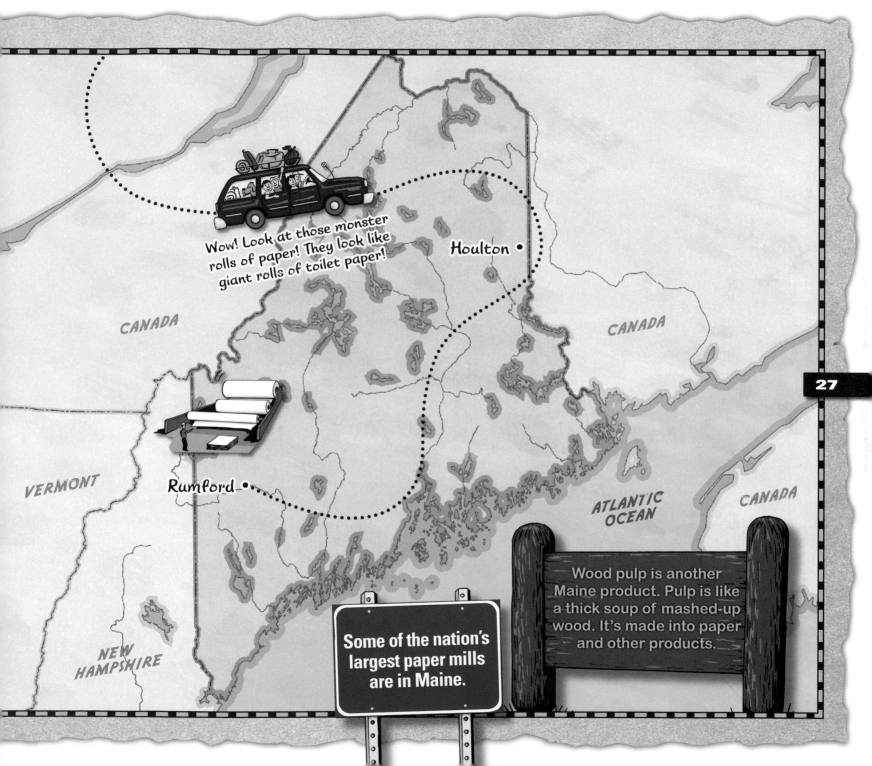

Wow! Look at those monster rolls of paper! They look like giant rolls of toilet paper!

CANADA

Houlton

CANADA

VERMONT

Rumford

NEW HAMPSHIRE

ATLANTIC OCEAN

CANADA

Some of the nation's largest paper mills are in Maine.

Wood pulp is another Maine product. Pulp is like a thick soup of mashed-up wood. It's made into paper and other products.

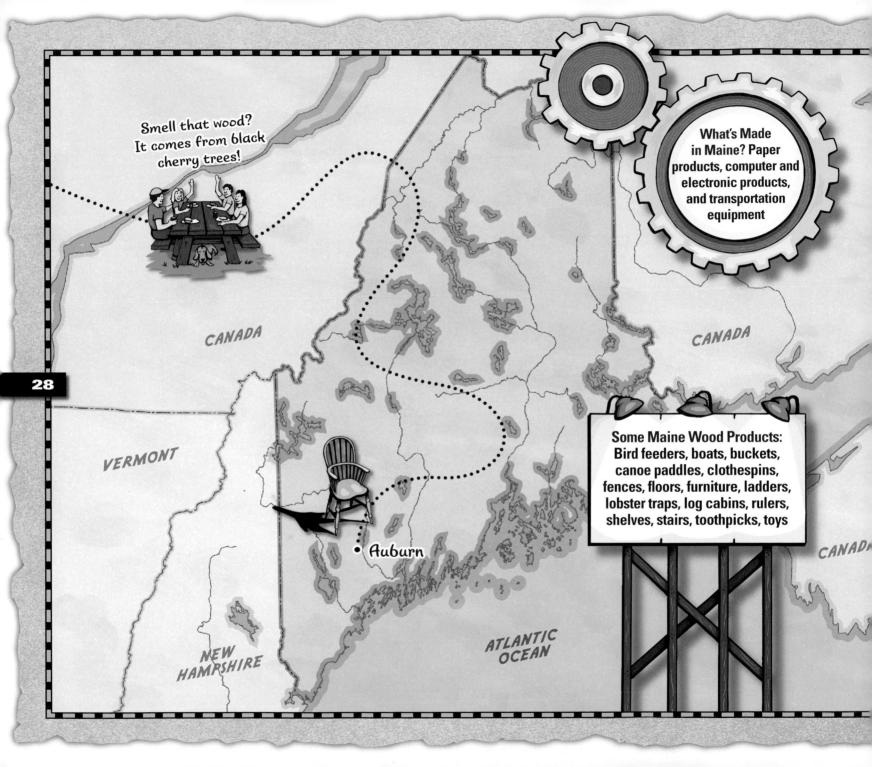

Smell that wood? It comes from black cherry trees!

What's Made in Maine? Paper products, computer and electronic products, and transportation equipment

Some Maine Wood Products: Bird feeders, boats, buckets, canoe paddles, clothespins, fences, floors, furniture, ladders, lobster traps, log cabins, rulers, shelves, stairs, toothpicks, toys

CANADA

CANADA

CANADA

VERMONT

NEW HAMPSHIRE

ATLANTIC OCEAN

• Auburn

Auburn's Wood Workshop

An Auburn craftswoman finishes a chair.

Look at your chair or desk. Were they made by machines? Probably. But visit Thomas Moser Cabinetmakers in Auburn. You'll watch people making wood furniture by hand. You'll see them cut, glue, and sand the wood. They end up with beautiful chairs and other furniture.

Maine's wood industry has always been important. Mills throughout the state saw logs into boards. Those boards might become houses or furniture.

Not all of Maine's wood products are big. Some are tiny. Maine is the toothpick capital of the world. It makes about 50 billion toothpicks a year!

What's Mined in Maine? Sand and gravel

Everyone's dressed up for the Acadian Festival. The cross stands where Acadians first landed in Maine.

The Acadian Festival in Madawaska

The Acadian Festival in Madawaska

Madawaska is the northernmost town in Maine. Just across the Saint John River is Canada! Most people in Madawaska are Acadian. Acadia was a French colony in Canada. The British drove the Acadians out in 1755. Most Acadians went to live in Louisiana. But some settled in Maine.

Now Madawaska holds the Acadian Festival every year. People act out the Acadians' arrival in Maine. Then comes a bean supper, music, and games. People wear Acadian costumes, and many speak French.

Acadians are just one of Maine's ethnic groups. Some Mainers have roots in England or Ireland. Settlers came from Germany, Sweden, and many other countries.

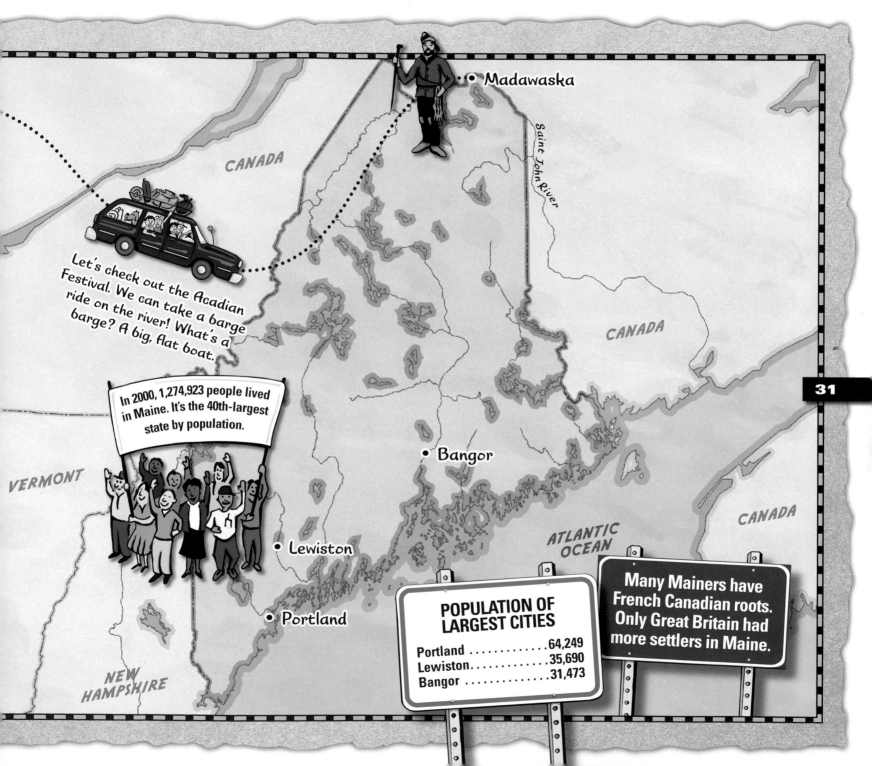

Madawaska

CANADA

Saint John River

CANADA

Let's check out the Acadian Festival. We can take a barge ride on the river! What's a barge? A big, flat boat.

In 2000, 1,274,923 people lived in Maine. It's the 40th-largest state by population.

VERMONT

CANADA

Bangor

ATLANTIC OCEAN

Lewiston

Portland

NEW HAMPSHIRE

POPULATION OF LARGEST CITIES

Portland 64,249
Lewiston 35,690
Bangor 31,473

Many Mainers have French Canadian roots. Only Great Britain had more settlers in Maine.

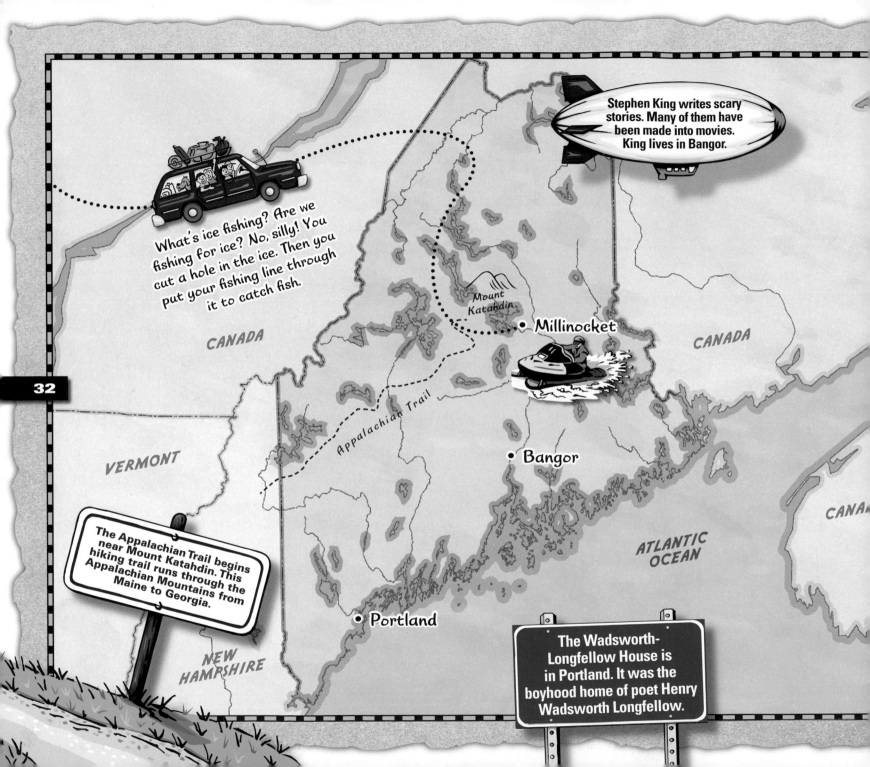

Stephen King writes scary stories. Many of them have been made into movies. King lives in Bangor.

What's ice fishing? Are we fishing for ice? No, silly! You cut a hole in the ice. Then you put your fishing line through it to catch fish.

Mount Katahdin

• Millinocket

CANADA

CANADA

Appalachian Trail

• Bangor

VERMONT

The Appalachian Trail begins near Mount Katahdin. This hiking trail runs through the Appalachian Mountains from Maine to Georgia.

ATLANTIC OCEAN

CANA

• Portland

NEW HAMPSHIRE

The Wadsworth-Longfellow House is in Portland. It was the boyhood home of poet Henry Wadsworth Longfellow.

The Katahdin Winterfest

These antique snowmobiles at the Katahdin Winterfest sure are different from today's machines!

Grab your sled for the kids' sled race. Go ice fishing with your whole family. Watch hundreds of snowmobiles in races and parades. Are you hungry? Try the pig roast or the spaghetti dinner. It's the Katahdin Winterfest in Millinocket!

This is one of Maine's fun winter festivals. Many other events celebrate fishing, boating, or food.

Mainers enjoy the outdoors. They go skiing or snowmobiling in the winter. In warmer weather, they enjoy swimming and sailing. Some people like climbing. They might climb mountains or rocky sea cliffs. It's great to look out from the top!

Meet Eartha, the Giant Globe

What a world! Before leaving Maine, get a good peek at Eartha!

Have you seen a globe of the Earth? Well, you've never seen one like Eartha. It's the world's largest **rotating** globe. It turns around just like our planet does.

You can see Eartha at Yarmouth's DeLorme Company. This mapmaking company built the globe. The idea was to fill people with wonder. They'd see how everyone on Earth is connected.

Suppose you wanted to hug Eartha. You'd need lots of other kids to help you. You'd all join hands around the globe. How many kids would it take? More than thirty! What a hug!

One inch (2.5 cm) on Eartha is equal to 1 million inches (2,540,000 cm) on Earth!

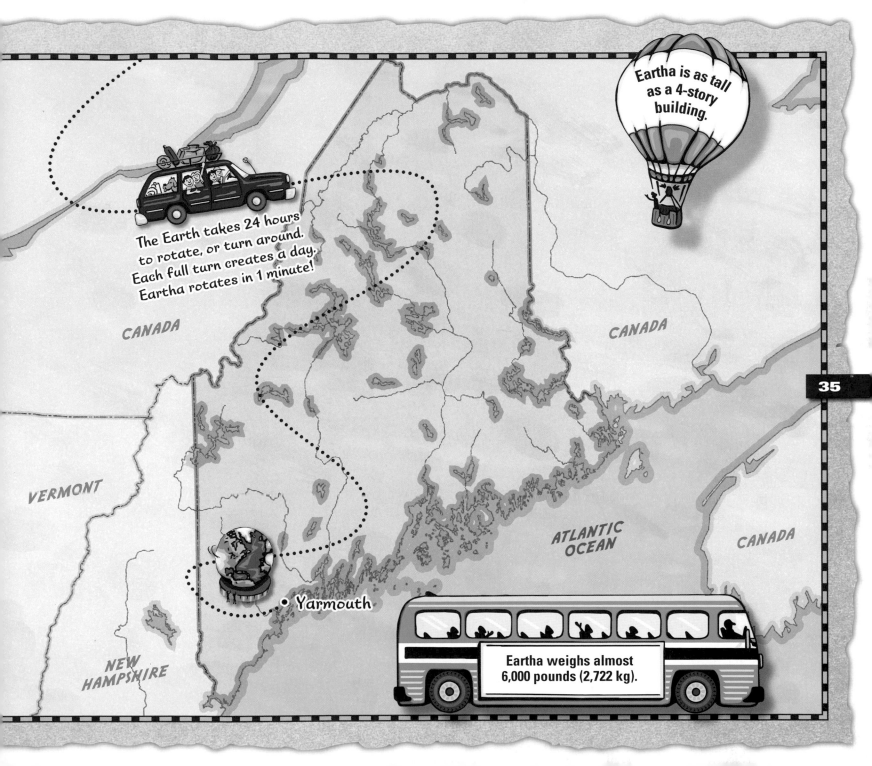

Eartha is as tall as a 4-story building.

The Earth takes 24 hours to rotate, or turn around. Each full turn creates a day. Eartha rotates in 1 minute!

CANADA

CANADA

CANADA

VERMONT

NEW HAMPSHIRE

ATLANTIC OCEAN

• Yarmouth

Eartha weighs almost 6,000 pounds (2,722 kg).

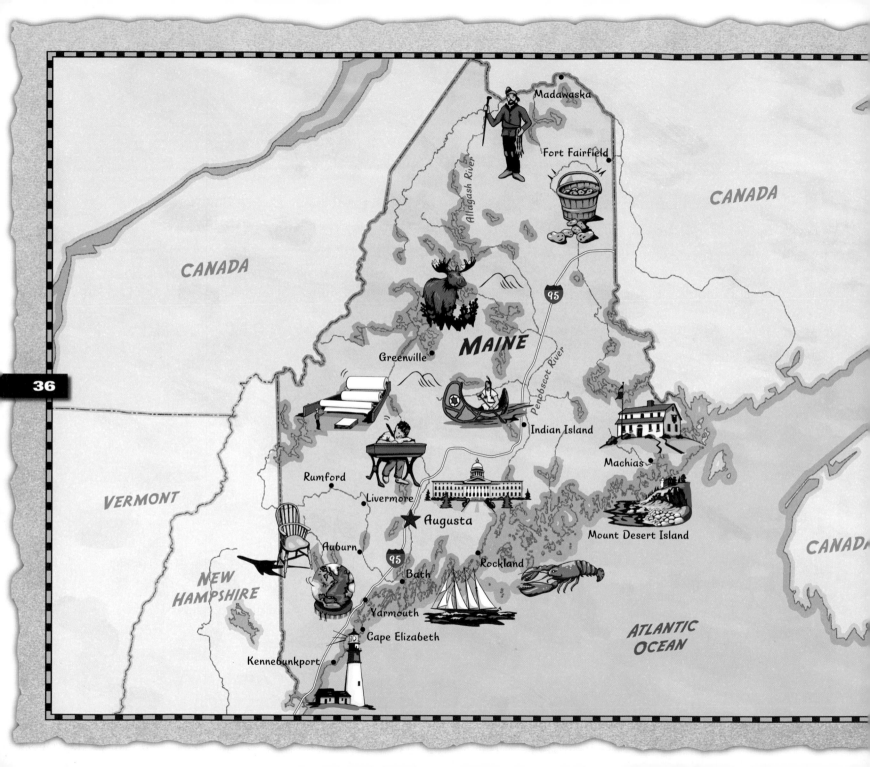

CANADA

CANADA

Madawaska

Fort Fairfield

Allagash River

95

MAINE

Greenville

Penobscot River

Indian Island

Machias

Rumford

Livermore

Augusta

Mount Desert Island

Auburn

95

Bath

Rockland

CANADA

VERMONT

NEW HAMPSHIRE

Yarmouth

Cape Elizabeth

Kennebunkport

ATLANTIC OCEAN

OUR TRIP

We visited many amazing places on our trip! We also met a lot of interesting people along the way. Look at the map on the left. Use your finger to trace all the places we have been.

Where is the Moose Stompers Weekend held? See page 8 for the answer.

What was the Old Gaol? Turn to page 12 for the answer.

How tall is Maine's tallest lighthouse? Page 18 has the answer.

What is a female lobster called? Turn to page 20 to find out.

Who celebrates Potato Feast Days? See page 24 for the answer.

How many people live in Portland? Look on page 31 for the answer.

Where does the Appalachian Trail begin and end? Page 32 has the answer.

How much does Eartha weigh? Look on page 35 and find out!

WORDS TO KNOW

agricultural (ag-rih-KUL-chur-uhl) having to do with farming

colonists (KOL-uh-nists) people who settle a new land for their home country

colony (KOL-uh-nee) a land with ties to a mother country

industry (IN-duh-stree) a type of business

maritime (MA-ruh-time) having to do with travel and work at sea

politicians (pol-uh-TISH-uhnz) leaders involved in government

reservations (rez-ur-VAY-shuhnz) places set aside for a special use, such as a home for American Indians

rotating (ROH-tate-ing) turning around on a center point

sap (SAP) a sticky juice that oozes from some kinds of trees

traditions (truh-DISH-uhnz) customs followed for many years

That was a great trip! We have traveled all over Maine! There are a few places that we didn't have time for, though. Next time, we plan to visit the Seaside Trolley Museum in Kennebunkport. Visitors can view the National Collection of American Streetcars. Trolley tours of the area are available, too.

More Places to Visit in Maine

Maine covers 30,862 square miles (79,931 sq km). It's the 39th-largest state in size.

STATE SYMBOLS

State animal: Moose

State berry: Wild blueberry

State bird: Black-capped chickadee

State cat: Maine coon cat

State fish: Landlocked salmon

State flower: White pine cone and tassel

State fossil: *Pertica quadrifaria,* a primitive plant

State gemstone: Tourmaline

State herb: Wintergreen

State insect: Honeybee

State soil: Chesuncook soil series

State tree: White pine

State vessel: The arctic exploration schooner *Bowdoin*

State flag

State seal

STATE SONG

"State of Maine Song"

Words and music by Roger Vinton Snow

Grand State of Maine, proudly we sing
To tell your glories to the land,
To shout your praises till the echoes ring.
Should fate unkind send us to roam,
The scent of the fragrant pines,
The tang of the salty sea will call us home.

Chorus:
Oh, Pine Tree State,
Your woods, fields and hills,
Your lakes, streams and rockbound coast
Will ever fill our hearts with thrills,
And tho' we seek far and wide
Our search will be in vain,
To find a fairer spot on earth
Than Maine! Maine! Maine!

FAMOUS PEOPLE

Bean, L. L. (1872–1967), apparel company founder

Bradley, Milton (1836–1911), game and toy manufacturer

Craven, Ricky (1966–), NASCAR racer

Dix, Dorothea (1802–1887), social reformer

Ford John, (1894–1973), film director

Fuller, Melville (1833–1910), U.S. Supreme Court chief justice

Hamlin, Hannibal (1809–1891), politician

King, Stephen (1947–), author

Longfellow, Henry Wadsworth (1807–1882), poet

Maxim, Sir Hiram Stevens (1840–1916), inventor

McCloskey, Robert (1914–2003), children's author and illustrator

Mitchell, George (1933–), senator

Morse, Marston (1892–1977), mathematician

Munsey, Frank (1854–1925), publisher and author

Piston, Walter (1894–1976), composer

Roberts, Kenneth (1885–1957), author

Samuelson, Joan Benoit (1957–), Olympic distance runner

Smith, Margaret Chase (1897–1995), politician

Tyler, Liv (1977–), actor

White, E. B. (1899–1985), children's author

TO FIND OUT MORE

At the Library

Austin, Heather. *Visiting Aunt Sylvia's: A Maine Adventure.* Camden, Maine: Down East Books, 2002.

Craats, Rennay. *E. B. White.* Mankato, Minn.: Weigl, 2003.

McCloskey, Robert. *Time of Wonder.* New York: Viking Press, 1957.

Reynolds, Cynthia Furlong, and Jeannie Brett (illustrator). *L Is for Lobster: A Maine Alphabet.* Chelsea, Mich.: Sleeping Bear Press, 2001.

On the Web

Visit our home page for lots of links about Maine: *http://www.childsworld.com/links*

Note to Parents, Teachers, and Librarians: We routinely verify our Web links to make sure they are safe, active sites—so encourage your readers to check them out!

Places to Visit or Contact

Maine Historical Society
489 Congress Street
Portland, ME 04101
207/774-1822
For more information about the history of Maine

Maine Office of Tourism
59 State House Station
Augusta, ME 04335
888/624-6345
For more information about traveling in Maine

INDEX

*Bye, Pine Tree State.
We had a great time.
We'll come back soon!*